Break The Cycle
with
The Ten Relationship Rules for
FamilyPower

AN ATTEMPT TO REDUCE THE ECONOMIC GAP
BETWEEN THE RICH AND POOR IN AMERICA BY
IMPROVING THE CHANCES FOR LONGTERM
SUPPORTIVE FAMILIES.

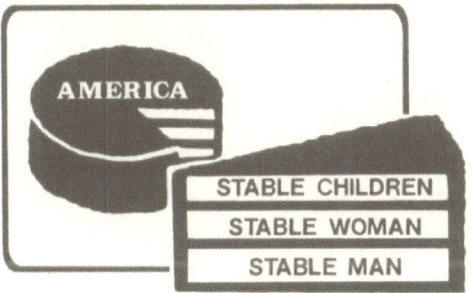

Break The Cycle

AMERICA

STABLE CHILDREN
STABLE WOMAN
STABLE MAN

Eric Harriel, Author

Copyright © 1989, Rev. 1991, 2011
Eric Harriel

ISBN 978-1-4583-4156-3

Table of Contents

About the Author

Eric Harriel is the fourth of six children born to Willie and Delores Harriel in St. Louis, MO. His family moved from the Pruitt-Igoe Projects when he was 4 years old. He appreciates having 3 older brothers; Reginald, Wayne and Cornel who kept him out of trouble with gang life, a younger brother, Vertice, deceased at age 24, and a younger sister, Crystal, born when he graduated from high school. He had very limited contact with members of other races during his childhood. His first Harrison Elementary

School principal, Mr Fisher, was white, the others were Black. He went to Pilgrim Lutheran Church which was predominantly white, but every other aspect of his life was predominantly black. His neighborhood went quickly from low to middle income, relatively safe, and predominantly white, to low to middle income, unsafe, economically depressed and 90 plus percent black. He is a proud graduate of Beaumont High School.

Like so many other people, he pointed the finger at the people from outside of his neighborhood as the reason for the negative turnabout. Then, he got a chance to get a closer look at how the people from outside of his neighborhood really are through an internship with Inroads, Inc. Inroads is a non-for-profit organization that prepares and places high school and college students in corporate internships of the major of the student. He concluded that these other people either had enough concerns of their own to not be concerned one way or the other about people in his neighborhood; or, they were looking for someone to point fingers at, also. He decided during his years at St. Louis University that pointing fingers at others as the reason for one's success or failure is counter productive.

After earning a BS in Marketing from St. Louis University, my goal was to be self-employed. I took many chances in the job market and relied primarily on sales, insurance sales and substitute teaching positions for income when my self-employment and ground floor opportunities did not work out. Like many other men who had completed school, I was becoming restless with the single social scene and was considering a change. This consideration caused me to conceive a child in 1983 and become married

in 1984. My son Eric II was born 4
months later.

Due to various reasons, my wife
and I separated in 1988 and
divorced in 1991. I especially
missed raising my son, Eric II on a
daily basis. Our time went from
daily, to three times a week, to twice
a week, to once a week, to a weekend
every two weeks during the times
I've had to travel out of town on
business. My first impulse was to
blame others for my particular
situation but due to my previous
experiences I knew that was not the
case and counter productive. I
married a second time. My second
wife had four children already and
lived in a small town in Illinois
where she remained very helpful to
me and her family. We amicably
dissolved that relationship after five
committed years of being together. I
am on my third marriage to a
wonderful wife and I have my grade
school age daughter Mareme.

Through long thought, much reading and many discussions with people from many backgrounds, including the ministry, the ideas of *Break The Cycle* were developed. The ideas have helped me to see where I could have been thinking differently and to see what needs to be accomplished. The message in *Break The Cycle* is intended to cross over income levels, religious beliefs, racial lines, job type categories, family status, generational differences, and neighborhood types. They are designed to concentrate on everyone's ability in America to overcome obstacles and to maintain the freedom we are born into. The ideas give every individual an opportunity to know of Relationship Rules designed to improve the probability of relationship and family stability.

Mr. Harriel has presented these rules on his own radio talk show in St. Louis, in presentations to

students of all ages and also, to
some adult groups such as The City
of St. Louis Health Department.

Worth More Than Silver and Gold

Men and Women are not the SAME
There is a Big Difference in the Body and
BRAIN
A Woman is about the business at HAND
She is the operations leader of child and MAN
A Woman can tell if you are playing or NOT
She will transform what you are thinking from
what you want to what you GOT
A Woman can handle a man, other women, her
household, the job, the children, her own
desires, and cook the STEW
Today's woman can also lock you up, operate
any business, put out any fires, and be the
primary breadwinner, TOO
A Woman does not need a man to tell her what
to DO
A Man who thinks a Woman is weak had
better find some other household to leave his
SHOES
A Woman appreciates a man who has spiritual
strength and keeps her PROTECTED
She does not need a man who thinks he is
some Messiah RESSURECTED
A Man who thinks a Woman's job is to make
him babies and be his HELPMATE
Is looking for a Candy Girl who is not worth
more than a fun DATE

That Man will not be respected and it takes a
good Woman to make a family and a man
GREAT.
He will not be respected by the Woman and
children and he will be looking for an ESCAPE

A Good Woman can do it all by herself and
leave the candy man and sugar daddy
BEHIND.
A Woman can be submissive or tell you
without a doubt what is on her MIND.
But when treated with the respect and the
dignity she Deserves,
A Woman shows the whole world she is worth
much more than the world's SILVER and
GOLD RESERVES.

Chapter One
INTRODUCTION

The number one problem in America is broken families. This problem is greater than topics such as drug abuse, crime, gangs, teenage pregnancy, unwanted pregnancies, infidelity, increased racial tensions, the spread of AIDS, public school crises, abuse of women, child abuse, public housing crises, homelessness, lack of hope, and so on. These problems have been with us for centuries, but they have escalated dramatically in recent history because of broken families. If the majority of families worked together long enough to raise the children to adulthood in a stable environment, the above list of problems would not be as devastating.

Statistics show that at least one out of two marriages end in divorce. We can expect-and, I'm sure, identify from the experiences of people we personally know that a

greater percentage of families aren't
really "working together" to raise
children to adulthood in a stable
environment. The divorce rate
above doesn't include "families" that
started without a marriage license
and the rate doesn't include the
legal marriages that broke down
long ago, yet the couple never
officially divorced. Unofficially the
rate of family breakdown is probably
at least 80 percent.

No one wins in a broken family.
The man feels divided and hurt. He
has to divide his attention and
resources between his own
necessities and desires and those of
his children who most often are with
the woman. Although most men
won't admit it, they still feel a
responsibility to the woman, too.

The woman feels an increased
burden. She now has to increase her
time and personal resources with
the children. Although she may
receive assistance from the man, it

normally doesn't make up for his absence. In his absence she feels solely responsible for the welfare of the children. It becomes difficult for her to trust fully another man with her children.

The children miss the care and attention to which they are accustomed. Now they have a part-time parent and an overburdened one. Children can feel the pressure when there is little family stability. They can tell when they are an intrusion on their parents' lives. Often they react in very unpredictable ways.

This is a cycle that is repeated in one out of two marriages in America. It is very destructive to the economy and morality of each individual, the family and the nation. It is destructive to the economy because it becomes much more of a struggle for men and women whether married or not to" do the right thing" which is provide for themselves and/or their family. Federal, State and local governments and charities have to do the providing. This Cycle is destructive to morality because it breaks up the sacred private and personal relationships between man and woman or between adult and child. People tend to feel as though their bodies, hearts and spirits are not special anymore.

Broken families is another reason for increased bitterness between the low to middle income and well-to-do. Well-to-do males are in control of the American economy but because of the civil rights and women's rights movements they have agreed to give up some control for the last twenty or so years. Their sons and daughters don't have it as easy as before because of sharing the opportunities with women, the low to middle income and minorities. At the same time they can see the low to middle income, women and minorities constantly asking and needing more government and philanthropic help.

Minorities and women on the other hand, have had greater opportunities for the last twenty years. However at the same time it has become more difficult for men, especially black men, to find gainful employment because of the greater acceptance of women in the workforce and minority women being counted twice in affirmative action quotas. Although the opportunities are better, the financial benefits are not redistributed efficiently because of broken families. The chances are even worse for a low to middle income husband, wife or child to develop their full potential because their families have never been in control economically.

63% of youth that commit suicide
   are from fatherless homes
(Source: U.S. D. H.H.S., Bureau of the
Census)
75% of all adolescent patients in
   chemical abuse centers come from
   fatherless homes.
(Source: Rainbows for all God's Children)
70% of juveniles in state-operated
   institutions come from fatherless
   homes
(Source: U.S. Dept. of Justice, Special
Report, Sept 1998)
80% of rapists motivated with
   displaced anger come from
   fatherless homes
(Source: Criminal Justice & Behavior, Vol
14, pp. 403-426, 1978.)
85% of all children that exhibit
   behavioral disorders come from
   fatherless homes
(Source: Center for Disease Control)
85% of all youths sitting in prisons
   grew up in fatherless homes
(Source: Fulton CO., Georgia jail
populations, Texas Dept. of Corrections
1992)

82% of teenage girls who get
   pregnant come from fatherless
   homes.
90% of all homeless and runaway
   children are from fatherless
   homes.
71% of all high school dropouts come
   from fatherless homes.
(Source: National Principals Association
Report on the State of High Schools.)

These statistics translate to mean
that when the father is absent from
the child's life, he/she is:
5 times more likely to commit
   suicide.
32 times more likely to run away.
20 times more likely to have
   behavioral disorders.
14 times more likely to commit rape.
9 times more likely to drop out of
   high school.
10 times more likely to abuse
   chemical substances.
20 times more likely to end up in
   prison.

20 times more likely to get pregnant.
(Source: Fathers' Support Center, St.
Louis, MO 63158, updated 2009.)

More Than Muscles And Money
        by Eric Harriel

A Man and Woman are not the same,
There is a big difference in the muscles
and brain,
A Man has more power to load a truck,
A Man has the imagination to create a fast
buck,
A Man has the skill to win a fight,
A Man has the spirit to know wrong from
right,
A Man takes responsibility for men,
women and children
A Man uses his money to create a home to
live in,
A Man is a parent regardless of the
mother's fitness,
A Man makes a difference in the life of
his children
Our past, present and future is the witness,
A Man is not superior to a woman, we
know that,

The job description is different, that's a
natural fact,
Some women call men names like boy
and hon,
But want men to act like men from sun to
sun,
We need responsible men in our homes
and community,
So why let the child support system take
away their
income, homes, children, legal rights and
other security,
Our communities know our men are
feared and oppressors
try to bend them,
More people from the community need to
be
employers, teachers, voters and jurors so
we can defend them.
Our communities don't even give our men
a proper Man, Mister or Sir,
Then we are surprised when our men call
each other the N Word,
A Man should know to lead his family
with love,
He can't lose if he gets his guidance from
the Creator above,

A Woman who thinks a man's job is to
give her money and
take care of her heavyweight,
Is looking for a big boy and not a
responsible mate,
The big boy becomes a man, the
relationship becomes hate,
She will lose every man and her children
may not turn out straight,
We Men can be as serious as a heart
attack and then be SO funny,
But one thing for sure we are much more
than muscles and money.
www.break-the-cycle.vpweb.com

Chapter Two
THE PROBLEM

So what causes families to break up? Let's look at the current ideal situation first.

What happens when both husband and wife are gainfully employed? They don't have children yet. They both go to work ideally at about the same time. They have the remainder of the day, off days, vacations and holidays to spend as they please. Their combined incomes could offer them the ability to start buying a home, start saving an emergency or opportunity fund, develop their careers to supervisor or seniority status or to develop a company of their own. Now, let's examine what other than not wanting each other could cause this family to break up. It could give us clues to solve the break up cycle.

First, one of them could want to change careers. Changing careers in some cases can cost time and money.

The one who wants to change careers may need to return to school while still working. This could involve daily and weekend study and classes. The couple may not be able to withstand the additional financial or time stresses. Or the career changer may need to stop or reduce work time or leave town for training. This too could create additional financial and time stresses.

Second, one or both of them could find their secure income threatened by a supervisor, strike, company closing or any other reason. This too could make the marriage intolerable.

If the best situation has a poor chance than there is little need to discuss in much detail the success potential of even less favorable circumstances. The other circumstances include marriages where only one is gainfully employed, a child or children are

already existent, they're renting
without considering buying a home,
they're not saving money, they're not
improving in their careers, they
have no religious convictions.

This is to say that a couple
starting their family with both
having jobs, even without children,
have a great chance for an
unsuccessful marriage. In these
days of department closings,
company closings and whole
industry closings, having a job is not
enough security to provide for
oneself or a family. Unfortunately
this society is telling people to start
providing for a family with no more
security than a job. This book
attempts to explain the benefits of
each family having a home, savings,
a successful career and time tested
coping strategies at the onset of
starting a family.

Chapter Three
THE SOLUTION

So what can be done to improve the chances for a family to bear fruit and multiply? How do you stop families from breaking up? Here is the answer. We cannot stop families from breaking up, but there is a much better chance for them to survive if five minimum standards are in place before the family is formed.

These five minimum standards will serve three purposes.

1. Make it possible for practically anyone, even a child, to objectively recognize when a couple is ready to start a family.

2. Helps each partner to recognize if their perspective mate is truly acting in both of their interests, because it is almost impossible to know what is in another person's heart or mind.

3. The five minimum standards would provide protection and comfort in times of family crises.

Stable Man

To solve the problem we should work in stages of family stability formation. First, make sure the man is stable. He should accomplish these five goals before marriage.

The Ten Relationship Rules For Family Power

Rule One

Don't take a marital type commitment from a man seriously unless he has made a commitment to get all the P-R-I-D-E components below:

Property Ownership – Real Estate with his name on the Title or ability to buy.

Resolve --Something he believes in that he can teach and lead others to believe, such as a chosen occupation, philosophy, belief, religion, art, sport, etc. A man should only have a woman who respects his Resolve.

Income -- Supervisory Position, Seniority Position, or Successful Business.

Dollars Saved -- At least 25 percent of income in savings.

Education—Minimum personal expectations of education goals achieved.

Rule Two

Don't take a marital type commitment seriously from a woman unless she has completed a commitment to get P-R-I-D-E components above or at least completed all the R-I-P-E components below:

Resolve --Something she believes in that she can teach and lead others to believe such as an occupation, philosophy, belief, religion, art, sport, etc. A woman should only have a mate who respects her Resolve.

Income --Seniority position, Supervisor position, Successful business or decision to be a Stay-at-home wife or mom.

Property Management -- Experience owning, renting or managing a place of residence.

Education Minimum personal expectations of education goals achieved.

Rule Three

T.E.A.M.
(Temporary Engagement to Achieve More)
Prior to a legal marriage, marital type relationship or engagement, a man or woman may TEAM UP(work together, live together, entertain together) or be INTIMATE (hand-holding, hugging, kissing and cuddling) with as few or as many people as they choose. We do not encourage premarital sex or shacking up.

However if people should go beyond abstinence, protection (to avoid sexually transmitted diseases, unplanned pregnancies and broken hearts) should be utilized at all times.

If attractive and popular celebrities cannot avoid the pitfalls of lying and cheating what makes us think we can?

Is your life or child's health worth taking a chance on?

The decision to commit to one's own self and to choose a committed partner requires clear thoughts unobstructed by less-than-desirable commitments, intimacy, and (Other People's Money) addictions.

Remember if it is the (other person's money). They can withdraw it at anytime for any reason.

Rule Four

After the P-R-I-D-E, R-I-P-E and T-E-A-M components have been achieved the couple should check the C-A-R-E list below before getting married, having a marital type relationship or having a child together:

Cooperate -- Does each mate try to move in the same direction as the other mate?

Appreciate -- Does each mate have consideration for the Resolve and value of the other mate? In other words does either mate take the other for granted?

Respect --Does each mate want to be with the other mate and values their Resolve, opinions and other qualities?

Encouragement --Does each mate actively try to stimulate the success of each other's Resolve and goals through words and action?
©Break The Cycle 2010

Rule Five

After the P-R-I-D-E, R-I-P-E, T-E-A-M and C-A-R-E components have been achieved the couple should check the C-H-A-N-C-E list below before getting married, having a marital type relationship or having a child.

Cook
Who is going to cook the meals, how often and what will be cooked? Who will take primary responsibility and how much successful experience does this person have?

Housekeeping
Who will take primary responsibility for keeping the home clean? What is the present housekeeping behavior of both?

Add income or value
If one person needs a little assistance, will the other help a little as needed? For instance, work part-time for a few months or fill-in as secretary or mover or accountant or driver, etc.

Nurse
Will each mate try to help the other through a health crisis? Will one mate

take charge of the family's health issues? Sometimes the family could be in-laws, aunts, uncles, brothers, shared children, not shared children, et al.

Caretaker of Children
How does each mate take charge of the needs of the children? How does each mate feel about each other's children? If an emergency arises will mates agree to take care of other children?

Entertainment
Does each mate satisfy the Entertainment needs of the other? Will the mate help entertain family, business associates, friends, etc. for various reasons?

Rule Six

A WOMAN should have the power over intimacy. INTIMACY is hand-holding, hugging, kissing and cuddling. A woman should not beg, force or ultimatum a man to be committed to her. Either a man or woman can be the primary provider.

A   Responsible   Woman   takes
responsibility for the needs of herself,
her significant others, other women and
is generally the primary caretaker of
children.

A Responsible Woman, adds input to
the rules, teaches the rules and is the
first level enforcer. A woman makes the
choice concerning intimacy both prior
to   and   during   a   marital   type
relationship.

A Responsible Woman, is usually the
Chief Operations Officer (COO) of her
family, second level rule maker and
second level spiritual & religious leader.

Rule Seven

A MAN should have the power over commitment. He must have completed the P-R-I-D-E components and only pick a R-I-P-E Woman.

COMMITMENT is the behavior of two people who are loyal to and take responsibility for each other. A man should not beg, force or ultimatum a woman to be intimate with him. Either a man or woman can be the primary provider.

A Responsible Man takes responsibility for the needs of himself, other men, women and children. A Responsible Man makes the rules, is the second level enforcer, second level teacher and interprets the rules.

A Responsible Man or Woman may have more than one mate prior to a marital type relationship.

A Responsible Man sets the parameters, such as, music, curfews, language, images, spiritual guidance, religions, etc. for the family. He also sets up the protection against predators and financial failure. He is the family Chief Executive Officer (CEO).

Rule Eight

A Candy Man is a man who has not completed the P-R-I-D-E components.

A Sugar daddy is a man who has completed the P-R-I-D-E components but who only wants a Candy Girl. A Sugar daddy does not want a Candy Girl to improve herself and will try to treat a R-I-P-E woman like a Candy Girl

An Amdur is a man with (Anti-Male Disorder.) His only interest is in what is good for women therefore he is not a good representative of manhood.

A Mookie is a member of the (Men only Klub.) He hasn't yet come to understand his responsibility to women and children.

Neither a Candy Man, Sugar daddy, Amdur, nor Mookie should get married, have a marital type relationship nor have children.

Rule Nine

A Candy Girl is a woman who has not completed the R-I-P-E components.

A Sugar mama is a woman who has completed the R-I-P-E components but who only wants a Candy Man. A Sugar mama does not want a Candy Man to improve himself and will not respect a man with P-R-I-D-E.

A Honeybee is a woman who draws a man to her with her honey but is very likely to sting him with baby mama drama and child support demands.

Neither a Candy Girl, Sugar Mama nor Honeybee should get married, have a marital type relationship nor have children.

Rule Ten

Men with P-R-I-D-E and Women who

are R-I-P-E should disregard the child support and child custody system set up by the government. They should obey the law but avoid the system.

Men should resist the oppression that forces them to be [child support payers and visitors] versus [responsible men who provide, direct, lead and take full responsibility for their children.]
Women should avoid the temptation to be manipulated by attorneys, politicians and government workers to take advantage of and revenge on the men of our communities.

The welfare/child support system encourages women to make extremely self destructive choices. These poor choices have the effect of reducing the supply of responsible men in the community and causing our children to be fatherless. This same system causes the men, women, children, schools and community to turn against itself and remain powerless. Responsible men and women make good choices and bear the consequences of the choices they make.

If at any time the man needs help to readjust because of serious problems, he can return to his parents for a short time before trying again. When he has accomplished the five goals he can find a wife who has completed the same goals above or who has at least completed four minimum goals (R.I.P.E.) with whom to marry and have children.

Let us begin with the understanding that it is the man's responsibility to keep the entire family unit together. The reason we say this is because most men don't want to take care of children on their own. Therefore they are willing to cherish and take care of a woman also, if necessary. It is also more socially acceptable for a man to be the primary provider for the family. On the other hand, most women expect to be the primary caretakers of children. They do not expect to have to take care of a man so they may be unwilling to indefinitely take care of him. Many females are taught to use and ask for the supposed extra strength (physical and financial) of a male and feel good about it. Furthermore many men don't accept very well having to be taken care of by a woman. Throughout his entire life a boy is taught to offer his supposed extra strength (usually physical and financial) to the female and make her feel comfortable in accepting and asking for help. When through some unfortunate circumstance he becomes the financially weaker vessel he doesn't easily adjust to the change. He often expresses his general discontent by being abusive to her or her children or by being irresponsible in other ways.

Our Maker has already allowed more time for the man to make preparation for a family. Unfortunately, most men have not taken adequate advantage of the available preparation time. What do we mean by men having more preparation time? Unlike women, men are not under the biological pressure for health reasons to have their first child at a young age. Specifically, a man has the biological capability to father his first child, without concerns with the health of himself or the child, even after the age of forty. On the other hand, women are advised to have their first child well before age forty in order to assure the health of the mother and child. For health concerns of herself and baby, a woman may want to begin a family before completely achieving the five goals as previously mentioned (The P.R.I.D.E. components) If she needs time to reach the five goals, it would relieve a good deal of stress if her husband has already successfully reached the goals.

Unfortunately many men after entering the work world waste a lot of time and money on apartments, cars, clothes, expensive women's gifts and entertainment. They intend to have a family someday but don't know what to do until that time comes. They feel they can start saving and start to buy a house when their income increases or when they marry and have the wife's income. Family, friends and community tell them that they are "supposed" to pay for their lady friend's needs, wants and indulgences. Even if they are not told this directly, they are often exposed to this way of thinking through television, movies, magazines, radio, etc. This line of thinking was appropriate when the line of thinking in society was the men were "supposed" to get the jobs. Now, since men are not "supposed" to get the jobs then men are not "supposed" to be responsible for their lady friends. This one change in attitude could afford men the ability to prepare for their own or their family's stability.

He does not realize that once other people are dependent on him a career change could be more difficult. He doesn't realize that once others depend on him he may not take a chance on a promotion or transfer within his company as easily. He may not realize that if she has to make any adjustments to her career he could experience extra financial and time stresses. He may not realize that once you get out on your own in an apartment it is not as easy to save for a house or anything else. He may not realize that his wife might question the amount of time he is away from home and not helping around the house when he very well could be attending to business.

Most men don't realize that their wives, who are just as capable as

them, want them to be more stable
while she is going through her
career and maternal changes. He
may not realize that starting his
own business may become an
impossibility because he cannot
afford to risk the family income. He
may not realize that he may not be
able to spend the quality time he
would like with his own children
because he has overburdened
himself.

Hard Head Heart Hero

A woman who satisfies a man's hard head
heart hero never has to be concerned
about being alone or being disrespected.
Her responses to his inquiries if done with
a symbiotic intelligence keep the
relationship and his mind protected.

A woman who satisfies a man's hard head
heart hero is always a part of his spirit
night and day.
His interests such as his family, dreams,
hopes, and business keep her in his spirit a
special way.

A woman who satisfies a man's hard head
heart hero is the pleasure even a best
friend and parents cannot equal.
Once the first experience has been
achieved there is no going back, what
never ends is the hard to refuse sequel.
A man loves the way a woman comes to
him to ask for answers away from the
congregation
A man loves it when a woman turns to
him when she experiences trepidation

A man loves it when a woman feels
comfortable enough to ask him to relieve
her of humiliation
A man loves it when a woman counts on
him for inspiration
When a man is chosen to be her hero, a
woman satisfies a man's hard head heart
and desire to be wanted and needed
forever with no expiration.

Stable Grandparents

Being stable is especially
important if they have children. The
grandparents don't have to
experience some of the
unpleasantness (disobedience, noise,
erratic behavior, and diaper
changing) of child-rearing again.
Often if a couple cannot lean on each
other for adjustments they lean on
the grandparents. The
grandparents' peace, retirement
plans or vacation plans could be
jeopardized creating instability
where there was stability.

Stable Woman

Second, we work on stabilizing
the woman. What are some of the
reasons a woman might attempt to
reach the five goals before starting a
family? What are some reasons the
woman may decide to at least
complete the previously mentioned
four R.I.P.E. goals before starting a
family? What are some of the
reasons a woman might want to wait
until her man has become stable to
get married? As she fully develops
her career or business she may have
problems. As she goes through
childbirth she may want some
dependable help. If she needs time
to adjust, she'll have a stable
husband to depend on. A woman
may have to take care of the
children by herself more often if her
man is not stabilized. She may feel
neglected if they cannot get together
because of competing family and
career goals. She may have to put

off having children until an age when she is biologically less flexible. She may feel compromised if he takes risks with the family income by starting a business, changing careers or continuing education. She may want to start a business but may not be able to because he is unstable.

She may not be able to take advantage of an opportunity for her dream home. Saving money is more difficult. Continuing education is more difficult. Enjoying a holiday, vacation, evening, or day off is more difficult. Once married you may be stuck with a man who is a quitter or excuse maker or a wannabe. Your family deserves to know if it has a man who is able to get a piece of the American Pie and keep it. Let's avoid wasting time and money on marriages to men who have not proven they can protect themselves from poverty.

She may have unknowingly set her and her family up for abuse or neglect by adding responsibility to a man who hasn't proven his ability to handle it. She may not realize that many men have big egos and not being able to take care of family necessities may be a threat to that ego. She may not realize that she could lose or alienate her wonderful man by not waiting until he is prepared for a family. Let's not put you or your children in a position where it is necessary to live with relatives, friends, shelters or neighbors.

Mama Drama In The Hood

Marva, why are you looking so cross as
I come in the house?
Do you think you should pick my
friends and tell me when to come
home?
I know what is waiting for me at home
and I know to rest before work.
If you keep looking at me so cross you
will be all alone.

Mama since Dad left you keep looking
cross at me when I come in the house.
Why do you always scream at me, try to
pick my friends and make me come
home?
I know you are looking out for my best
interest
When I get on my own I will set my
own time to come home.
Sweet (baby) Mama why do you look so
cross when I come home?
You are the love of my life, we have
children, and a loving home.

You keep bringing up marriage, but we
have been together for a while
If legal marriage is your only option
then we should have held hands only
until we walked down the aisle.
We can have a wedding type ceremony,
same last name, honeymoon, and
shared assets without allowing the
crippling child support, tax, credit
slavery systems' fingers
around our necks.

Sweet (baby)Mama why do you look so
cross when I get home?
Do you think you know what is better
for me than me, I am grown?
I can pick my own friends and I need to
rest before work that I can figure on my
own
I hear white women treat a man with
respect and are mindful of their voice
tone.

Mama why do you look so cross at me
when I come in the house?
Since dad went with that white woman
you can't even look at me straight

I don't feel welcomed in this house
anymore
And Mama I am coming out the closet,
so please don't hate.

Mama why do you look so cross when I
come in the house?
I am the man of this house and you had
better be nice.
Bring in the money, cook my food and
wash my clothes
And if you think about having a
boyfriend you had better think twice.

Stable Children

Thirdly we'd work on stabilizing
the children. Parents who both have
achieved their goals or at least one
has achieved the goals will be
available to support, counsel,
discipline, instruct and supervise
their own kids. Kids will learn a
respect for authority, property,

family and community. As this
system continues, mother and father
will begin to prepare children for
adulthood and family earlier. The
actualization of the five goals would
be sooner.

The age difference between a
stabilized man and a woman who
has finished school and started a
career would be smaller. For right
now it may be necessary for a young
woman to be with a man who's a
little older. Actually many young
women are opting for men older
than themselves now.
Unfortunately many of them had
already contributed to the instability
of several young men before
realizing they wanted a stable man.
Hopefully this book will help them
to recognize this earlier.

Body Games
By Eric Harriel

If you treat your body like a
bargaining tool,
You can expect to be treated like a
gardening tool,
It doesn't matter if you're poor or
rich,
It doesn't even matter if you're
legally hitched,
If you dance to the music, you must
pay the piper,
Unless you like being used like a
toilet room wiper,
Old habits are hard to break,
Knowledge can help you avoid the
same mistake,
Male or female, it's all the same,
You don't get respect if you treat
your body like a game.

Chapter Four
WHY HAS THE INCIDENCE OF BROKEN FAMILIES INCREASED SO MUCH?

The following three events contributed to the increase:

1. The greater acceptance and appreciation for women in the workforce.
2. Affirmative action quotas that count minority women twice.
3. Welfare Programs became the Child Support Programs.

These adjustments altered this society in tremendous ways. In the last twenty or so years men must compete with women to get employment at all, not to mention gainful employment. Women have been known to perform as well as or better than men, but often don't demand as much compensation.

They can accept less because often family members, the government, or the man in her life can supplement her expenses. Also a woman will often accept an unlikely entry-level position, such as secretary or clerk, and move up in the company from within. This is competition which men had not been accustomed. Twenty years ago when the man could not find gainful employment, the family suffered through it together. Now when the man can't find gainful employment, the woman takes care of the family.

Another primary contributor to myopia is the Child Support System. It is directly derived from the welfare system. The welfare system was paid for by government taxation and had policies that would not provide for a family with a man included. Therefore many men had to leave their families for the good of the family. The men had to fend for themselves. The welfare system started letting those who never had a man in the family receive benefits, also. That started females having children just so they can get welfare benefits such as housing, food, education, employment, WIC, and medical care assistance. The welfare system became so large, and a negative influence on the community, that the welfare system was finding it difficult to pay the welfare families and to maintain its own payroll. Therefore the welfare system during the Bill Clinton Presidential Administration was forever changed. The major reason was to rid communities negatively affected by a surplus of nuisance fatherless children. But another reason was to relieve the government of the responsibility of providing checks to the needy families. The fathers were used as scapegoats supposedly to pay the household with the mothers and children. However since the statistics clearly demonstrated that average income earners need two incomes to provide financially for one household. The child support department had to know average and below average income non-custodial parents could not provide for the custodial household. However, without the responsibility to provide for the needy families, the child support system can use the hundreds of millions of tax allocated money for its own purposes. In effect the child support system only helps one-third of its constituents receive extra income. Thus the child support system fosters the need for itself and primarily serves itself. The child support system as a solution is worse than the problem it is supposed to solve. In fact it creates three bigger problems. 1. Because it drives a bigger wedge between the parents over money that does not exist. The fathers and mothers of the children do not cooperate or respect each other. 2. It keeps the non-custodial parents so broke and legally oppressed that they cannot fend for themselves. 3. It separates the children from both parents. The mother is asked to do the job of two parents. She often has to work two jobs. The fathers are asked to provide for two households with average and below average incomes. The focus goes from doing what is best for the children to finding money to make up for the money sent to the other household.

There is Legislation called Shared Parenting making its way through the legislatures. It is designed to presume equal custody for both parents without child support payments. Learn more at www.acfc.org the American Coalition for Fathers and Children.,

Consequently, most men do not remain in a family where they have to be supported. There are two reasons for this:

1. Women do not expect to take care of a man for any duration of time.

2. Men do not accept very well being taken care of by a woman.

"Most irritating of all to Kunta and his mates, though, was how the second-kafo girls with whom they had grown up were now so quick to remind them that they were thinking already of becoming wives. It rankled Kunta that girls married at 14 rains or even younger, while boys didn't get married until they were men of thirty rains or more." (From Roots, by Alex Haley).

HOPE
Believing you can make it in spite of the opposition.

Chapter Five
A FEW ATTITUDE CHANGES

A few needed attitude changes
are all it would take to break the
cycle of family break ups in this
country. We should change the
attitude that a man with a job is a
good candidate for a husband. A job
isn't enough. We should change the
idea that a man should try to have
children at a young age so he can
play sports and take children on
activities with more vigor.

If a choice had to be made, do
children need more activity from a
father or do they need more stability
and direction? We should change
the idea that a couple who genuinely
cares for each other should get
married. We should develop a
relationship normal that gives
couples a chance to explore many
mate options simultaneously in
order to make better informed

choices. We should change the idea that two people of the same age are good marriage candidates. With the extra time men need and have comes extra age. With the shorter time women have comes less age. Currently the age gap between an accomplished man and a woman with no kids entering the workforce is not small but the age difference should reduce with better future planning.

We should change the idea that since a baby is born to a couple they should marry. A baby is not enough. That man should support and supervise his child but he will remain much more valuable if he uses his time developing fully for family responsibilities. We should change the idea of men and women needing to move out of their parent's home soon after they start working. They can contribute to their parents' home and begin saving much better while staying with the parents versus wasting money on an apartment.

We should change the idea that it is cute to see a young couple struggle through their first few years of marriage. The noble institution of marriage is the backbone of our civilized society. It should not be a source of humor anymore.

This is not a new idea. It is only an idea that needs to be reintroduced. There is too much emphasis on government help and professional counseling. We have heard of the adage, "An ounce of prevention is worth a pound of cure." We are now paying for cures.

Let's reduce the need of the government to pay so much to enforce child support payments. If men knew absolutely it was not time for them to have a wife or children, they might be more responsible.

Let's reduce the need for government welfare programs. If

women knew that the men they
were dating were absolutely
unsuitable yet, they would be more
careful or choose better.

Let's reduce the need for marital
counseling fees. A marriage with a
financial and spiritual foundation
does not need as much counseling.

Let's reduce the costs of legal and
court fees for divorce, child custody,
division of assets, etc.

Let's reduce some of the hospital
costs of husband and wife trying to
destroy each other because of
outside pressures. Let's reduce the
hospital costs of abused, neglected,
and poorly raised children, as well
as the costs of children being
mistreated by parents, stepparents
and guardians.

Let's reduce the costs of the
destruction caused by children who
are neglected.

Let's reduce the costs of buildings
and land left unattended because

families cannot afford to purchase them.

Let's reduce the costs of men and women going to prison because they become anxious to achieve higher goals, but do not see a realistic/legal way to achieve their goals.

Let's reduce the costs of school busing because with strong stable families, children can get a good education in their own neighborhood for several reasons:

1. It becomes less of a struggle for either parent to achieve their respective goals, therefore, they can attend parent-teacher meetings; volunteer their time; join the school board; or assist their child(ren) with completion of homework.

2. Children of stable families should have higher goals because they would have constant role models in their homes.

3. The teachers and principals could have higher expectations of the children since the parents and the environment would be more stable.

4. Because of greater participation in ownership, there should be more money available in the area to assure that only premium facilities and staff are at schools.

Stop Anti-Male Bigotry

I have a personal story that shows how unhealthy our attitudes have become. I was indicted for "failure to pay child support and criminal neglect." It was not true. I took care of my son Eric II as often as practically possible.

From age 5 he lived primarily with his mother during the school year. He lived with me on weekends, during the summer and some school sessions. It was the most practical arrangement without disturbing his school schedule. Both of his parents, although divorced and separated, directly provided for his housing, food, clothing, supervision, etc. like nature planned it.

Encouraged by the child support system however, his mother filed for late child support payments. My priority was providing for my son directly. Sometimes I did not have the money to help her take care of her portion of the responsibility.

The case went to court in St. Louis County in June 1995. I also was trying to get primary custody at that time. I was tired of being the most absent parent. Eric II was showing signs of needing more of his father's influence. All the evidence presented showed that I was taking care of my son directly. My son's performance improved in school and in the home when he was in my custody. I had legitimate reasons for not paying support. I lost every case and was given a 90-day jail sentence and a Class D felony conviction.

To this day there are many employment opportunities I cannot take advantage of because of the felony conviction. I think employers should not be allowed to bar someone from employment based on a non-related past conviction. After all, the criminal justice system is not perfect. A determination by a court merely settles a case. It does not necessarily mean a person is innocent or guilty. The general public needs to change its attitude from making sure a child receives child support money to making sure a child is directly provided for by both parents. A child receiving support is still living in a fatherless home. Review the statistics, earlier page.

Chapter Six
RESPECT EACH OTHER

Let's not refer to a young child as a baby. For the child may delay becoming independent of others.

Let's not refer to a teenager as a young child. For the teenager may delay accepting responsibility for his actions.

Let's not refer to a 21-year-old as a teenager. For the adult may delay preparing for his or her own independence.

The terms "young man" and "young lady" are what a teenager is called so they may behave as an adult. These terms are an insult to anyone over age 21. It's as if the speaker is saying, "I am more superior to you regardless of your age or status in life."

If we want our adults to take on the independence and responsibility of adults than we need to refer to them as adults. If you don't know the name of a man and he is over age 21 the proper communication is "man" "mister" or "sir" and for the woman it is "woman," "miss" or "lady." For example: "May I help you, miss?"

"Mister does that envelope on the floor belong to you?" "I was taking this man's order."

Just as it is not proper for an adult to call another adult "young man" or "young lady" it would not be proper for the younger adult to be discourteous when correcting an older adult about the incorrect reference. For example the younger adult might say, "Excuse me sir, I mean no disrespect but I don't mean to be disrespected either. I prefer to be called man, mister or sir instead of "young man." Becoming 21, an adult, should be an honor. It should not be an opportunity for the often-said remark; "You're just a baby." We should embrace our new adults every year and welcome them into the ranks instead of treating them like unwanted competition. We should also freely share with them some of the responsibilities of being an adult. Do you think we have a better chance of influencing the development of responsible adults by insulting them or encouraging them?

Unfortunately, with the current level of disrespect, many people once they become over age 21, feel that to become accepted as adults they must look older, move slower or act older. Often they purposely pick up weight, stop taking as much care of their looks, start growing facial hair, engage in cussing and swearing, learn to consume strong alcoholic drinks, waste money on apartments or get married or have babies before being prepared. It should not be necessary for potentially attractive and energetic people to look older than their actual age just to be respected as adults.

Conversely, there are many people over age 21 that refuse to try to look or act older. They often aggressively demand respect or don't care if they are respected at all. Neither is a good choice. Why should a person have to rebel just to get respect?

In summary, if we as a society gave respect promptly to all adults, then perhaps the new adults would not exhibit destructive behavior to be respected. How can you expect children to respect adults when adults don't respect adults?

Respect Pledge

I pledge

To respect all people

Unless they treat me illegally,

Immorally or disrespectfully

Because they have information,

materials and wisdom

which can benefit me

and which they may not share with

me

If I disrespect them.

Chapter 7
SELF DESTRUCTIVE COMMUNITY BELIEFS

Some of the problems in our communities are caused by the beliefs we hold that have been influenced by the news media and other people who have no interest in improving our communities. Specifically I'm referring to the child support and custody practices and the monogamy practices of our community before marriage.

First, I want to discuss the child support and custody practices. I say practices because the laws of our country and many of the states are well written and protective. However, it is still true as Dr. Martin L. King, Jr. said," the greatest crime of mankind is the crime of doing nothing." When men are being separated from their children for doing nothing more than being born a male, our community, and specifically our attorneys and preachers make no effort to help these men. These courts openly discriminate against the male parent 80% of the time.

Even female parents with little or no means of supporting herself get custody preference over men who do support themselves. Men are expected to take care of themselves and their babies when they have custody and are expected to take care of the children when they do not have custody. Usually for a man to get sole custody, the woman has to be unfit, unwilling to keep the children or dead. Women are only expected to take care of the children when the children are in their custody. Men are expected to pay child support even when they have very little income, for instance on unemployment security or in jail. The men have to make up for any missed time making payments. A parent with custody of the child who goes through an economic challenge does not have to make up for the regular income shortfall. I DON'T UNDERSTAND why there has to be a child support payment when both parents are ready and willing to share the custody and responsibility of the children.

If a woman is adult enough to choose a man. If she is adult enough to choose a man to marry. If she is adult enough to have a baby. If she is adult enough to split up with a man, then she should be adult enough to take care of the responsibility of herself and all the children in her household. If she is not adult enough to be the head of a household, then why is she given custody of children? Another point I don't understand. These women come on these talk shows like "Maury Povitch" claiming they want to find out who is the father of their baby. There might be two or three choices. My question is what kind of woman or girl has unprotected sex with that many men in such a short period of time? Why does the public support the children being raised by an admitted irresponsible person? If she is not considered irresponsible than maybe our standards are too low. Perhaps these real low standards in the community are the reason the pimp business is almost non-existent.

Average women act like prostitutes. The community is producing too many irresponsible women who aren't made to take responsibility for their behavior.

Speaking of irresponsible behavior let's go to the other practice I mentioned above that is destroying our families and communities. It is the belief that monogamy is the only accepted relationship. Once a couple pairs off they are expected to see only each other. I can understand monogamy in marriage, but we also have monogamy before marriage. I will submit below the reasons I

believe this practice causes very
negative behavior in our
communities.

Reason 1:
Most communities still believe
the man is supposed to ask the
woman to be his wife. There is a
shortage of "good men." As long as a
woman has the attention of a man
she doesn't have to adjust to his
ways. She only has to keep him
from leaving her. What do you
suppose is the number one way that
women in many communities keep
their unmarried men from straying?
Yes, you guessed it; she must be
intimate with him. Intimate is
hand-holding, hugging, kissing and
cuddling, and it works. The entire
community would label him as a dog
if he were even seen with another
woman. What happened to the
man's choice as to with whom he is
to marry or go steady? Unless he
can pull away from his guaranteed

source of intimacy in a way that
doesn't expose him as a dog, he is
stuck with the woman who chooses
to be intimate with him. So now the
race is on. Women are in a hurry to
be intimate with a "good man" as
soon as she can to keep him from
making any decisions on his own.
What happened to the man choosing
his helpmate? Once enough time
goes by he is pressured by the
community to marry the woman
with whom he is intimate. He is
expected to take full responsibility
for his decision, however in many
cases, he only made the decision
that he wanted intimate behavior.
The woman who is able to be
intimate with him first and keep
him, along with the community
made most of the decisions.

Reason 2:

Women who have passed their prime with respect to good looks, or who are single mothers, or who are not generally considered attractive or who have non-adjustable attitudes have little to no chance of securing for themselves the few "good men" available. Often they make decisions they might not normally make if men were allowed to respectfully choose more than one woman with whom to have a relationship at a time. Some of those decisions include, lesbianism, childlessness, child bearing with a donor male, sleeping around just for fun with unworthy men, sleeping around for money, having affairs with taken men, or trying to force a happy situation with unworthy men.

Reason 3:

A man who is not entirely satisfied with the woman he is with will make other choices. But what choices does he have? Most women with self-respect in our communities will have nothing to do with a man who still has a relationship with another woman. So, the man must get a little satisfaction or variety from less-than self respecting women in the community. Throughout our communities so-called self respecting women are without a man. At the same time many "good men" are wasting their time and money on women walking the streets, looking for a fling at a club, or dancing at a booty club. If men could respectfully see more than one woman then there could be better pairings of good men with self-respecting women. For example, the unmarried but taken football coach who is such a positive influence on the son of a woman. The coach and the woman are obviously attracted to each other. However, she must raise the child alone and he is wasting his time and money with the neighborhood tramps. Remember, neither of the two wants to risk ruining their reputation. However, the stakes are too high. He could risk being exposed to a nasty disease, nasty companions of the loose woman, loss of money and loss of reputation. She could risk losing the positive direction her son has taken because of the coach. She could waste her time exposing herself and son to unworthy men. What happens when he stops being his coach?

This rule that man can only have a relationship with one woman at a time is a man-made rule. It is not consistent with other practices and expectations we have in our communities. Many people point to the Bible as their moral guide. However, the Bible does not say that a man can only entertain one woman at a time. In fact the Bible shows many examples of men having responsible relationships with more than one woman at a time. Look at the story of King Solomon, one of the wisest men of the Bible. King Solomon had more than one wife and his kingdom was one of the finest known to man. Our communities expect the man to take the responsibility to be head of household. However, he is given no authority to fulfill his responsibility.

If his helpmate decides to not cooperate with him than many of the men in our communities are the ones forced to leave the household. What kind of headship is that? Does the CEO leave if the second in command decides to not cooperate? Does the school principal leave if the assistant principal doesn't do the job well? A real head can promote, demote, hire, and give a raise to anyone under his leadership and responsibility. A token head has no real power. Although for many years it was unfair to other members of the family, men could abuse, abandon, or cheat on the family with no negative repercussions. Now, none of those practices are available to a man. We need to allow a man to choose more than one woman so his leadership would not be token, it would be real. I feel the monogamous relationships would have a better chance with this second option.

Please don't think this option is all about helping men. It is designed to help the entire family. Women would have better choices. Men would have better choices. Children would get better examples from the adults in the community. The Natural Selection Process which encourages mating among the strongest of the species will be allowed to prosper. We would reduce the growth of whores, lesbians, gays and whoremongers in our communities.

I would even go as far as suggesting we rename our mates.

For example if a man and woman pair off she is his woman and he is her man. If she is all the woman he wants or needs he can call her his wife, a promotion. However if she is not all the woman he needs he can get a second woman, (hire,) with the full knowledge of the first woman. Physical housing is not as important as the spirit. For example, he may live primarily with his woman because his children live there, however his wife or other woman may live in a different house. Any other arrangement is possible as long as there is honesty and trust among the participants. (Honesty and trust is a new idea in this day and age.) A man may initially call a woman his wife, but if she fails to meet up to the expectations, he could call her his woman, (demotion,) and call the second woman his wife. Of course none of this can be done if there is a legal marriage. Therefore, I suggest the community respect both *legal and non-legal marriages until the law respects multi-partner heterosexual marriages*. Some states now respect homosexual marriages. Which would promote healthier family relationships, laws that respect heterosexual marriages or homosexual marriages?

If we as a community agree to the above changes, how does it affect the choices of women? Will women be second class citizens waiting for men to make all the decisions? No! Women will have even more positive choices to make. Men like Bill Cosby, Jesse Jackson, Magic Johnson, Bill Clinton, George Peach and others could spread their positive influence respectfully like King Solomon.

As I said earlier, the community generally wants the man to take responsibility for his woman and his children. However, women do not have to take responsibility for men if they choose. Above you might notice there is no mention of men having the choice to abandon or divorce his wife, woman or children. However when a woman no longer respects or loves a man she may leave him. She may just discontinue living in the same residence and continue to have a relationship with him or she can leave him entirely. She doesn't have to decide to divorce him unless she desires to unite with another man.

Since men and women are different and are treated differently with respect to the law, the woman shouldn't be able to get a second man but she should be able to leave a man for whom she has no love or respect. For example, if her man decides to choose a second woman, she may separate from the man if she chooses. If they have children, as long as both parents agree to take care of the children there should be no child support rewarded. After some time has passed she may be

able to get him all to herself again.
However less damage to their
relationship could be a result of
respect for multi-partner
heterosexual relationships.

F-Fathers
A-And
M-Mothers
I-Involved in the
L-Lives of
Y-Youth

Chapter Eight
WHAT CAN BE DONE NOW TO ACHIEVE THESE GOALS?

1. Look at people now who are considering getting married. Let both the man and woman know the advantages of waiting until he has all the P.R.I.D.E. components and she has either completed the P.R.I.D.E. or R.I.P.E. components (This idea hopefully will appeal to one or both of their mental and emotional needs).

2. Look at marriages that have been unsuccessful. In some cases with the understanding that their choice of getting married at that particular time was a good one at that time, based upon the information they had. They may understand their ill feelings were only because of outside pressures. They may realize that the base problem could be solved and they can resume their marriages or not

be afraid to start over with a new partner.

3. Look at marriages that are successful. In many cases inordinate amounts of pressure are on one of the spouses. With the proper knowledge and planning the marriage should remain successful.

4. Look at the children. Make sure they know how beautiful marriage can be if both parties are properly prepared. Let them know why mom was overstressed at times and daddy was not there sometimes. Let the boys know they must achieve all their goals before babies or marriage. Having a baby or getting married will slow them down or stop them from achieving their goals. Let the girls know that they can achieve their goals alone, but it would be much easier on them if they have dependable help. Also, who wants to be alone? Ask the

children. Who would be a better
father to them than their own father
would if he has achieved his goals?
Who would be a better mother to
them than their own mother would,
if she is not overburdened and if she
is achieving her goals? The children
could probably see the benefit sooner
than many adults could.

Chapter Nine
EXPECTATIONS
Nothing happens overnight, but
what can be expected from these
attitude changes in the years to
come.

1. Fewer women should be on
welfare or poor single mothers.
Family and peers would
encourage women's involvement
with men who are reaching for
the five goals. Men on their same
level of achievement would be for
friendly associations, until the
men are achieving the five goals.

They would not consider
marrying or having a baby with
men unless these men prove they
can take the challenge of getting
a piece of the American pie.

2. There will be more
responsible, financially stable
men available from which
unmarried women could choose.

3. Fewer men paying alimony
and child support to a household
from which they get no direct
benefit.

4. Women living longer with
healthier minds and bodies
because they can relax more
knowing they have dependable
help to accomplish their goals and
raise a family.

5. Men living longer with
healthier minds and bodies
because they did not bear so

much responsibility without preparation. Their careers are stable; they are more attractive because they are competing for younger, less burdened women.

6. More companies being started
   For several reasons.
   A. Men have more time to start a company or two without risking family income.
   B. Women get the opportunity to more comfortably realize their full potential or start a company in spite of changes and childbirth.
   C. Children have both parents to give them the encouragement to accomplish goals greater than working for someone else.

7. Less dependence from the government on all levels because the family unit revitalizes and supports itself.

8. Neighborhoods would be safer.

A. With more men and women buying homes in their own neighborhoods versus renting, the tax base would increase.

B. There would be more people concerned about property values. There would be fewer renters in the neighborhood, some of whom do not care about property values or family safety.

C. With more concern for neighborhood safety and value, more businesses could survive because people would better see the need to keep money in their own community.

D .More responsible people could see the need to control the activities of local businesses and residences. There is an overabundance of lounges and liquor stores in many residential low-income communities. The presence of these factors on the community creates too many opportunities for neighborhood crime. Laws could be passed to limit the number of lounges and liquor stores in any residential area.

Laws could be passed to limit the number of businesses that stay open past a specified time in any residential area. Authorities could better control crime because the areas that create the better opportunities for crime will be reduced per residential area. These suggestions can only be accomplished when families are meeting the five goals.

9. Less drug addiction. There would be less drug addiction

because families could become involved sooner when they realize a family member is having a problem. If necessary, the family member in trouble could be transferred to a different, financially secure relative's house in order to change his sphere of influence: If necessary, the family could afford proper early counseling and treatment for the member in trouble. Hopefully, with more stable families there will be fewer potential victims for drug sellers.

10. Less homosexuality. Although there are some people who have no choice but to prefer the homosexual lifestyle, there are many that had a different choice. For several reasons they became homosexual. One reason is that they may not have experienced enough positive two-parent family role models. The

cultivation of accomplished, stable families would solve that problem. Another reason is that when men and women are unsuccessful in their first attempts at independence, they are often criticized or shunned by the opposite sex and their own families because of their temporary setback. Often there is a financially stable homosexual person who will help the criticized and/or shunned individual when everyone else turns his or her back on the individual. Often the homosexual will help the failed person, seemingly with no strings attached. As time moves on, the shunned individual finds him or herself accepting in the mind the homosexual lifestyle. Acceptance of a person as they are, is easier when that person is offering assistance. Once the subconscious mind accepts the concept of homosexuality, then one drunken, high or emotional moment could mean the difference between the conscious body also accepting homosexuality.

To avoid the acceptance of the homosexual lifestyle, parents might consider making the return to parents' home emotionally, as well as financially acceptable. The third reason that people might become homosexual is because of imprisonment /isolation. The solution is to keep people out of jail. If their parents are stable, individuals have less cause to go to jail. With stable families, law enforcement can be properly monitored. If men and women have a set of goals to accomplish, their minds could be less idle; therefore, they could reduce the likelihood of getting into trouble.

11. Less racial tension. The United States is truly a liberal and remarkable country. Everyone has an opportunity to reach his or her full potential. Unfortunately, many people born in America seem to take opportunity for granted, failing to take full advantage of opportunity. We spend too much time pointing fingers at others when we do not succeed. That is the problem between the low income, the well to do and different races. If the majority of people in this country were achieving their goals there would be fewer racial problems. The ten percent or less of people with mental imbalances who stir up dissention would soon be "I"nstitutionalized, "I"ncarcerated or "I"gnored. If everyone is realizing his or her goals, we can give the mentally imbalanced the

"I" signal (three middle fingers in the air).

12. Less teen pregnancy. The best advice to give young girls and boys about birth control, and venereal disease is to stop any physical contact other than hand holding. Advise these young people that if they touch more, than hand-to-hand, they could have an unwanted pregnancy or disease. Once the physical stimulation is experienced, no amount of logic or judgment can stop the passion. If you have never been physically stimulated than you cannot miss the physical stimulation: "You cannot miss what you never had." If you have been stimulated physically you may not experience pregnancy or disease the first couple of times, but you might have to make a conscious effort to avoid the temptation. You would be better

off using your conscious mind to improve other aspects of your life. Being aroused intimately is like taking drugs.

Intimacy is hand-holding, hugging, kissing and cuddling. Many people have no better control over their desire for arousal than they do for a drug as potent as cocaine. People jeopardize their future, family, friends and life for intimate arousal just as much as they do for cocaine. If you are smart enough to know the consequences of cocaine addiction, than you should fear the consequences of an addiction to intimate arousal just as well.

13. Less abortion. If you "choose" to allow more than hand holding, you "choose" to take a chance of becoming pregnant. Once you "choose" to allow more than hand holding, the "choice" is not yours

to destroy the life that your decision produces. The ability to bring a life into this world in a safe environment where that child has a tremendous chance to survive is a gift. We should not take this gift lightly. If men and women made the "choice" of only holding hands until they met someone who was "prepared" for a commitment then there would be less of an abortion issue.

A woman should be able to choose what happens to what belongs to her. But, if I am living in her house, she does not have the right to have that house destroyed until I am safely out. By the same token, a woman should be able to do as she pleases with her body, but only after the fetus' body is safely out.

Abortion for convenience is like giving one person the right to have an innocent life killed if they want to. What is ironic, is that abortion for convenience is in the same country where it takes twelve jurors, a judge, two lawyers, a bailiff and a court stenographer the right to have a person killed who is accused of being guilty. How can we make it easier for a life not accused of any wrongdoing to be killed than we make it for a person accused of wrongdoing? The unborn child should at least have the benefit of a courtroom of people, too.

If a woman insists that she wants an abortion so the baby will not have to grow in crime and poverty. Then, the nobler course of action might be for her to take out a cheap $100,000 term life insurance policy on herself. Have the child. Name some responsible couple as the child's trustees in the event of her death. If she truly believes that living in poverty and crime is not worth living, then she should be able to find some way to lose her own life. The woman, the couple and the child might be better off if that woman didn't have the ability to make decisions that respect life. If she believes life is worth living, she can use available resources to recognize her contributions to her previous problems and to change her present and future conditions. I hope she chooses to respect all life.

Abortion is allowing one individual to decide if another innocent individual shall live. No person or group of people should be able to decide if another innocent individual or group of innocent persons shall live. When it comes to innocent life, we all should be careful about protecting it. Because the next innocent life that might need to be protected might be your own or your families. Practically any family in America can retrace its roots and discover a time when innocent people from their own ancestry were chosen to be killed.

Free Registration and Criteria Waiver to All K thru12 School Staff
Relationships First

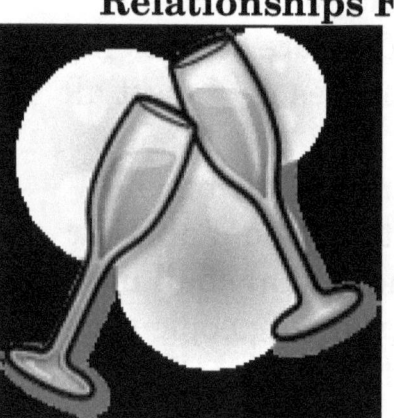

We want you to have a meal with at least four people individually each month for at least a year. Sometimes a friendship is developed. And sometimes there is a match of the two people we introduced. The point is the excuse that a person doesn't know

<u>Responsible</u> people will be eliminated.

This method reduces spending too much time alone with the wrong person and then settling because you have made a premature commitment or had intimate relations.

Male Criteria	Female Criteria
at least 4 parts	at least 3 parts
P R I D E	R I P E

"Men and Women who meet the above criteria would like to meet you."

Call if this sounds like something you would like to try.

Chapter 10
Church /Nightlife Conflict

The next step is giving people some other positive direction for their weekend/nighttime activity.

A problem experienced by many churches is the loss of its members from the period of high school until these persons reach early adulthood. A possible reason for this loss of potential members may be the conflict between being a member of an organized church, and participation in nighttime/weekend activities. When people finish a week of school or work, they want to celebrate, and socialize and mix and match. Seeing the problems created by nightlife, the majority of churches put down such activity.

Organized religion recognizes the dangers of men and women losing their composure around people who might want to take advantage of

them. Yet, obviously, the churches
are not offering satisfactory
alternatives. The late night
revivals, the volley ball games, night
Bible studies, midweek church
services, choir practices, etc. are not
filling the void after a week of school
or work.

The years when people stop going
to church are detrimental to society.
Usually when adults finally return
to church, much damage has been
done. Consideration must be made
for: previous and current destructive
relationships; the needs of their
children; persons who need to
control their addiction; persons who
have been incarcerated; persons who
have developed unhealthy attitudes
about sex or persons of the opposite
sex; family bonds that have to be
mended; actions that have to be
forgiven; opportunities that must
again be created. The church
spends an inordinate amount of time
counseling on problems that could

have been avoided in the first place. Once more we have the old adage, "An ounce of prevention is worth a pound of cure."

After going to the nightclubs, many persons with religious beliefs feel guilty about what they did the night before. Their hair or skin smells like smoke, and they do not want to be questioned about their previous night's activities. Also, they may be too weak to get up from bed on Worship mornings because their minds and bodies are weakened from alcohol consumption and/or lack of sufficient rest.

The solution is for there to be public nighttime/weekend activities for adults where they can celebrate, socialize, mix and match. However, take out the negatives. Take out the smoking, alcohol overindulgence, the lewd music and other lewd entertainment.

The establishment could operate like the current public

weekend/nighttime operations. This establishment should operate year round because once people start socializing in this manner, you do not want to be responsible for them going to the traditional establishments. This type of establishment should be large enough, or ample enough in numbers to accommodate the number of people who might be attracted to them.

Replace smoke-filled air with freshly scented air. In addition to alcoholic drinks add drinks with fruit and vegetable juices, soft drinks, non-alcoholic bar drinks, and special waters. Establish alcohol drink maximums to discourage over consumption. Offer fresh salads, steamed foods, fish, poultry, etc. Replace lewd music with dance music, slow music, jazz, and a greater variety of music. Replace lewd entertainment with plays, music groups, comedians, debates,

magicians, etc. This type of
establishment could influence two
generations: First, the generation
over twenty-one who are old enough
to go out at night. It would be nice
for them to spontaneously be able to
meet with people from outside their
usual circle of acquaintances, family
and friends. Secondly, it could
influence the generation of
teenagers who want to emulate
adult behavior. This group of
teenagers often feels as if its parties
are childish. This group may be
easily influenced to drink alcohol
excessively, smoke and engage in
lewd activities at an early age
because these activities may be
widely displayed by the adults
within their environment. Reducing
the desire to do the destructive acts
done by adults is another way to
"Break the Cycle."

Another benefit of the
nighttime/weekend entertainment
place is for the exercise. Men and

women do not look very appealing if at their ten-year high school class reunion they look twenty years older than they actually are. People are not drawn to the church or other acceptable places when they see young adult members who do not look healthy.

Church members will help the church, schools, social organizations, etc. much better if they are healthy. Even if a person cannot motivate him or herself to exercise properly, that person might be motivated to go out dancing. Dancing is a good form of exercise. Dancing is also a non-threatening way to meet someone. The type of establishment we are proposing could be beneficial to a wide variety of people, including: The alcohol drinker or smoker who wants to stop; the health enthusiast who wants to party or dance; the school teacher or administrator who wants to give a good example; the person with religious convictions

who wants to attend church; or
anyone else.

Chapter 11
CHURCH REFORM COULD
SAVE OUR COMMUNITIES

The African American
Community is a mess. There are
those who are doing well financially,
yet the spirit of the entire
community is so poor. It is an
embarrassment to see so much
potential go to waste. Regardless of
how many African American faces
are put into a position to solve these
problems, if there is not a logical
direction no progress is made. The
line of leadership that is the closest,
most accessible, and most influential
in the African American Community
is the Church. Even non-church
goers and members take their clues
with respect to community
standards from the Church. The
definition of the church for most of
the African American Community is
the building labeled with the word

"church" or a cross, led by a minister and attended by families and individuals every week. The Church has a seating area, a plan for passing along spiritual messages and spiritual songs. This is the concept of church either through a direct communication or through osmosis. This concept of church may be one of the reasons the African American Community is in such a mess.

Supposedly the Church gets its direction from the Bible. Yet, the Bible teaches explicitly that this is the type of church that Jesus disapproved. What is the church described in the Bible? The Bible says beware of those who preach on the street corners. The Bible says the church is where two or more of you gather in God's name. The Bible says Jesus turned over the tables of commerce that went on in the church. The Bible says Jesus was persecuted by the Pharisees and

Sadducees, the people who thought they had the right concept of church and would not listen to Jesus tell the truth about the scriptures. The Bible says the man is supposed to be head of his household, yet the Church assumes the spiritual leadership of households even though a capable man is in the household. The Church also approves or says nothing of the divisive practices of the court. The court orders child support and visitation for fathers even though the child, mother and father would be better served by giving respect to the households of both the father and mother. This policy causes many fathers to lose headship over their children and mothers to do a function intended for two parents. If the Church standards were from the Bible its members and the general community would make better voting and jury decisions.

I would like to see mature, responsible and spiritual men and women come up with a more correct, reasonable and non-confusing concept of church. I have some ideas and I would like to hear yours as well. First, I would like to explore the concept that church is the gathering of two or more people in God's name. Why must church only be in a building that says "church" or has a symbol on it? I'm sure when the Christians were being persecuted by the Roman Empire they were having church wherever they could. When Jesus had church he had it wherever or whenever he could. I would like to see every nightclub adopt a preacher. Ask a preacher to give a five-minute live or prerecorded teaching every night at 8pm, 9pm or 10pm to the guests. The preacher is not to receive any money, give his name or give the name of his church building. A real minister would not pass up an opportunity to teach to a group of people. Remember the answer given by Jesus when he was found fellowshipping with tax collectors.

Second, the Church takes tithes and offerings supposedly for the church, yet the church members see little of these funds. The finance company, the utility companies, the pastor and his workers share most of the tithes and offerings. I think the concept of church we have been taught has been robbing us of our resources and dignity for too long. The Church is the church members. I think a tithe exchange would be more correct in order to share resources of those who have a little bit more with those who have a little bit less. This is how it is done. Members of the community who work at least 30 hours per week give ten percent of their earnings to the tithe fund. The tithe fund is divided by the number of people who contributed. Each member receives an equal share. For example, if the equal distribution is $60 per week those who earned $300 per week will receive more than their $30 tithe. Those who earned $1000 per week will receive less than their $100 tithe but will receive something. I think it would encourage the spirit of giving and receiving in the community. I also think it would encourage better free-will offerings to support ministers and buildings.

Third, I would like to see the community place more of an emphasis on providing a church building and pastor primarily for widows, orphans, single women and men who desire spiritual uplifting versus for an entire family. A family lead by a spiritual head of household having home church whenever they want should be just as respected as the Community Church family. As the Bible teaches, you cannot serve two masters. You will love the one and hate the other. There are many women in our community who love their pastor but can hardly stand their husbands. The current system has to be confusing to the children. Should the children follow the spiritual direction of their father who has to make unpopular decisions, doesn't sing or speak well, only dresses well on special occasions and doesn't look comfortable, doesn't know important people, doesn't get as much respect from other adults including his mother and visibly falls short of the pastor's interpretation of the teachings of the Bible? Or, should he follow the spiritual direction of the church pastor who performs his practiced sermons and songs very well, is seen only on special occasions, and has the support of many people? Should our grown men be looking for a father (pastor), or should they be practicing and improving their own father (pastor) skills?

The current Church and pastor system is still very much needed. Families can continue to fellowship, choir practice, and have weddings, funerals and gospel concerts at the neighborhood Church Building. Families in the community who don't even attend the Church could be encouraged to contribute to a Church dedicated to widows, single women, orphans and men who desire spiritual uplifting. The Church needs reform. Don't expect the Church to make these changes. The Church gains money and power by the current system. It would earn more money and more power with the system I propose. However, I'm sure the Church will adhere to the philosophy, "A bird in the hand is better than two in a bush." Or the other philosophy, "If it ain't broke don't fix it." Although the current system keeps our communities and families in a constant state of weakness, the

Church will not change. Like the
Pharisees of the past, they are the
tradition keepers of today. However
if you would like the African
American Community to gain
greater power and spirit, begin
implementing these strategies in
your own life. All of these strategies
are being used in our communities
already, but on too small a scale.
You don't have to wait for a law
change, a large sum of money or
approval from anybody.

If you keep doing things the
same way and expect different
results than you meet the definition
of crazy.

Christmas is a Day of Joy

Christmas is a day of joy,
Especially for a little girl or boy.

Early morning on that day,
They open their presents and start
to play,

Some really young children don't
know what it means,
Just play guns, toys, games and
things.

Even some adults don't understand,
That Christmas represents the birth
of a man.

A man called Jesus who shows us
the way,
To live and prosper each and every
day.

Chapter 12
TRIBUTE TO MICHAEL JACKSON AND OTHER LEADERS WHO ARE NOT PROTECTED OR RESPECTED

Michael Jackson has shown tremendous courage as a leader of not only the African American Community but also the World Community. He has not done it in speeches; he has done it in actions and song. Review the songs Beat It, Bad, We Are The World, Off The Wall, Dangerous, Black or White, Give In To Me, Keep The Faith, Man in The Mirror, History, Blood on the Dance Floor, Invincible, Jam and on and on. The common thread is to take responsibility for your actions and don't let anybody push you around.

If our communities could increase these components by 20% our communities would become a better place. The courage shown by this man is being assailed by the enemies of freedom and ignored by the people with the least freedom. For example, Michael was accused of sexual molestation and he has been beaten up and left for dead by the people who control the media. Hundreds of priests have been found guilty of sexual molestation and the media blitz has been relatively small and there is little call for punishment for the Catholic Church which is a partner in the crime because it hid the crimes for so long. I cannot say Michael Jackson is not guilty, however, he should not be punished any more or less than The Catholic Church.

The beginning of the outright assault on Michael Jackson began when he made the song, "They Don't Really Care About Us." It should have shown to the world with whom Michael is aligned. Regardless of his appearance, there should be absolutely no doubt if anyone listens to the words of this song. In addition, it appears more than a coincidence that Michael along with his brothers, The Jackson 5, produced songs that also even now could be of great value to our communities. A few of these songs are, Got To Be There, Sugar daddy, Daddy's Home, Could it be I Stayed Away Too Long, Maybe Tomorrow. These songs can be used to express the relationships that we have with each other or possibly should have with each other.

Michael Jackson is strong. It is evident in a song on his latest CD titled, "Chosen One." The message is clear that he knows he has a mission. Just like Jesus Christ who sometimes wanted to be relieved of his burdens, however he knew he had to bear them for others. Michael Jackson has done volumes for the World and especially for the

African American Community. It is a shame he is being left to die. This is perhaps the reason there is little effective leadership in the African American Community. The real leaders feel they will not get supported or protected either. Other leaders on this list include, Nelson Mandela, Martin L. King, Jr., Malcolm X, James Brown, Muhammad Ali, Jesse Jackson, Bill Cosby, Bryant Gumble, Adam Clayton Powell, Jr., Magic Johnson, Bill Clinton and many more.

Michael Jackson is gone now. Nobody is perfect. However he left a legacy of music , videos and good will that carries messages of strength, determination, love, mutual respect and devotion that I pray will be repeated and influential until the end of time. And may past and future leaders get the respect and protection they need.

SUMMARY

To Break The Cycle of worsening
problems in America, we must
create more stable families.
Families have a better chance to
remain stable when families start
with stability. We should encourage
men to develop stability before
starting a family.

1) own a place of residence 2) save
25% of one's income 3) firmly
establish a career 4) develop a
religious conviction and 5) achieve a
minimum education goal. We
should encourage women to at least
1) finish school 2) start a career and
3) develop a religious conviction and
4) manage a household, before
starting a family.

We should encourage parents to
make the return after failure of their
adult children both emotionally and
financially acceptable with the

understanding the return is to be of short duration.

We should encourage the cultivation of romance by "hand holding only" when courting the opposite sex before one is "prepared" for a family.

We should encourage the participation by concerned adults of nighttime/weekend social establishments that don't allow excessive alcohol, smoking, lewd music or entertainment.

We should address people over 21 as adults to encourage responsible behavior.

All of these solutions do not require new legislation, taxes, loans, bond issues, votes, or education to be implemented. They only require the spreading of this message and a new attitude. We cannot stop broken families but there is a much better chance for them to survive if the five goals are in place. If the family owns the home, they have options available if a crisis occurs, i.e. stay longer, rent the home out, sell the home or borrow from the home. If the family has a year's income saved they have a few more options if a crisis occurs, i.e. supplement income with interest earned, borrow against the account, withdraw the money or start a business. If the family has a religious conviction they have more options if a crisis occurs, i.e. look to the religious doctrine, consult with the head of the religious order, or consult with other members of the faith or prayer. If the family has a firmly established career it has more options when a crisis occurs such as changing companies, starting a business, borrowing money because of credibility or taking a demotion.

What is probably more important is you have two people who have a better picture of each other and what is expected of them individually before they start a family. They have acquired some of life's necessities and can now put their love for each other as their number one goal. These two people have individually achieved a certain necessary level of growth and have reduced the chances of growing apart. .

THE SOLUTION IS IN OUR HANDS

"My son, do not forget my teaching, let your heart keep my commandments for length of days and years of life full of peace will they add to you." Proverbs ch.3 v.1

"Trust in the Lord with all your heart and lean not on your own understanding. In all your ways acknowledge Him and He will direct your paths." Proverbs ch.3 v.5

"Drink waters from your own cistern, running water out of your own well." Proverbs ch.5 v.15

"A good man leaves an inheritance to his children's children, but the wealth of the sinner is stored up for the righteous." Proverbs ch.13 v.22

"It is better to live in the corner of a housetop than to share a house with a contentious woman." Proverbs ch.21 v.9

"It is better to live in a desert land than with a contentious and fretful woman." Proverbs ch.21 v.19

"Educate a child according to his life requirements; even when he is old he will not veer from it" Proverbs ch.22 v.6

"The rich rule over the poor and the borrower is slave to the lender." Proverbs ch.22 v.7

"Do you see a man wise in his own eyes? There is more hope for a

fool than for him." Proverbs ch.26
v.12

Break The Cycle
By Eric Harriel

We know there are problems in the
American Community.   That is not
the QUESTION
For the way to solve these problems,
here is ONE SUGGESTION

Break the Cycle of family break ups;
Stable families can solve these
PROBLEMS.
Teach the men to be stable first,
then the women, then the
TODDLERS

Give adults an alternative to the
lounges and the BARS.
Teach young adults how to spend
wisely, versus on rent and
EXPENSIVE CARS.

Let us again learn to respect the
guidance of our RELIGION.

The choice of going to worship on a particular day, is each person's DECISION.
Teach parents with adult children to give them a little more TIME..
The time spent at home preparing to be the owner of life's necessities, could keep three generations out of a BIND.

We cannot afford to let the problems in the American Community to become any WORSE.
We should all work on helping our men and women to become a stable family of one FIRST

A simple message to our men would go a long way to relieve our STRESS,
Before starting a family, you should buy a home, save at least 25% of your income, profess your religion, and make sure your career and education IS A SUCCESS.

{back cover}

Unfortunately many men after entering the work world waste a lot of time and money on apartments, cars, clothes, expensive women's gifts and entertainment. They intend to have a family someday but don't know what to do until that time comes. They feel they can start saving and start to buy a house when their income increases or when they marry and have the wife's income. Family, friends and community tell them that they are "supposed" to pay for their lady friend's needs, wants and indulgences. Even if they are not told this directly they are often exposed to this way of thinking through television, movies, magazines, radio, etc.
{back cover cont.}

This line of thinking was appropriate when the line of thinking in society was the men were "supposed" to get the jobs. Now, since men are not "supposed" to get the jobs then men are not "supposed" to be responsible for their lady friends. This one change in attitude could afford men the ability to prepare for their own or their family's stability.

"It is better to live in a desert land than with a contentious and fretful woman." Proverbs ch.21 v.19

Let's not refer to a 21-year-old as a teenager. For the adult may delay preparing for his or her own independence.

www.ingramcontent.com/pod-product-compliance
Lightning Source LLC
Chambersburg PA
CBHW051424280526
45785CB00003B/1146